Loco Motive(s)

Poetry, Prose and Randomness
by
Michael Janflone

ISBN-13: 978-0692202326
ISBN-10: 0692202323

DEDICATION

To all of you out there that have had
a collision with me, and inspired me
enough to put pen to paper, or slap
typewriter ink onto whatever scrap
was lying around at the time, thank
you.

To those of you who encouraged me to
share my strung together words, the
most heartfelt thank you, especially
Daniel Singh.

CONTENTS:

ACKNOWLEDGMENTS

Too many to name, too many to thank. Everyone's time is coming in print but for now - God, family, friends.

Prelude-
Sludge Sundaes

What is a poet? An unhappy person who conceals profound anguish in his heart but whose lips are so formed that as sighs and cries pass over them they sound like beautiful music.

-Soren Kierkegaard

These are some pretty old poems, when I really had no idea what I was doing, other than doing drugs and passing time.

This is the first thing I ever wrote:

4 Random Lines With Specific Ends

Wince, waist deep, sewage stew could have been....
For two that looked perfect as one
Forever finite, send it back it's overdone
Final Jeopardy, Potpourri - "It's a many splintered thing."

7-2-1994

Breakage

Words, over the phone no less...
Must be kidding it's come to this...
Planning the big come down...
With me sitting far away
In my own dreams
Everyone always worried
What would happen when the bond breaks
Light the fuse, watch it draw closer and
closer
A snap, crackle, and the itch pinches blood
blisters
She wants a life spate
Puppy dog in tow and truth is...
I am devastated
Pick up the dynamite and throw it at you
Break me and I shatter every bit of life
I build indestructible dreams
I take her to spite you
Throw her in your face, sexier, younger
Makes me feel above the pain
All the while memories pull me down
A lot of years invested
Promises of forever exist in tight boxes
The pigeon's neck snaps while another
appears
Cruel magic, a vindictive trick
Wear some guilt, can pencil you back into my
tomorrow
Exact some revenge
I am not this reactionary...
Becoming something unsettled
Waves of agony constantly wash in

Can't dam an ocean, can't twist a tide
So I find the ebbs and subtle flows
Find my private island, deserted
All alone until I find my heroine

6/23/1995

Migration

On a misguided quest for static build up
Want my watch to run backwards
Erase today by getting back to yesterday
Need a compass to point south
The winter is coming
And I am tired of living in the icy chill
Want your hatred to love me
Want my love to rage
Would any of this make it all right?
Smile again, from the inside out
Wear the damage inflicted like a perverse
boy scout badge
Fucking me to protect others, that leaves me
baffled
Unravel the dream, your words a surgeon's
scalpel
Ignorance has never been bliss
But every cut non-vital, blood loss means
eventually the tank's empty
It all falls apart around me, everything in
pieces
Can't stand to just watch, so I invite you
back in
But I'm still not smiling
Give me a fork and a bowl of soup

My watch keeps ticking forward
A future ever approaching, creeping into
the present
Blink and another day has been lost
Uncomfortable telling you any of this,
But my soul flew south for the winter
And now the freeze
Locked , Lost
And so far away
Time now decides to stand still

Foster home

Disciple without the discipline
Mind lacking the proper comprehension
Passive servitude trips up a proper effigy
Nothing really around worth burning
Everyone equally deserving
Lacking enough fuel for a methodical
extermination
Boredom stuck up my conscience
Sold out souls stuck searching for spare
parts
Already drew the map for the junkyard
Looks eerily familiar
Maybe a bit to infinite to decipher
Forced to stare down the same dark street
Where I became the asshole that you know
There is no place to turn
Everything is missing from the future
Follow me if you must
You might just end up satisfied in the rot

Perfect parasitic passion
Hate blooms and happiness follows
Never look back now
Embrace the fog that obscures the visions
Revel in sucking life out of the dying
Become strong
So you can end me

2/4/1998

Familiar Stings

That seed buried deep, takes root.
Something isn't quite right.
Cause I've got this desire to shoot.
Tie off real tight.
Veins popping out.
The syringe loaded with my truest friend.
Slide it in, & I forget what life's about.
I'm slowly tripping towards my end.
I just don't give a fuck.
Out of excuses & out of luck.
It's all fading away so quick.
My candles burned out its own wick.
Think I've been here before.
Yeah I know the score.
I'm down.
I want to drown.
Can't see the end.
Too late, I'm around the bend.
Goodbye....

10/22/1998

A SHIFT LOCK CONFESSION IN 1999

SLIP-KNOT, CHOKE
NOT THIS WAY...
PAINT SMEARS
TOO RED, TOO REAL
SLIDING.
DOWN.
WHY TOUCH ME?
THERE?
I WAS SO YOUNG.
YOU WERE OLD
WISE...
I HATE YOU. RIGHTEOUSLY.
YOU TAUGHT ME TO FIGHT.
JUST NOT YOU.
THIS IS OFFENSIVE?
I'M COLD, I'M SHALLOW.
SIN. YOURS EMBEDDEDIN ME.
FUCK.
YOU MADE ME LAUGH SO I WOULDN'T CRY.
YOU SCARRED ME.
I'M A VIOALTION OF TRUST.
DAMNED TO REMEMBER
MY FACE BURIED IN SHAME.
WHERE'S THE RAINBOW ?
WHERE'S THE SUNSHINE ?
THE WATERFALLS?
THE INNOCENCE YOU STOLE
FUCK YOU BARRY

PART 1:
BLOOD

Poetry is thoughts that breathe, and words
that burn.

-Thomas Gray

Pork and Beans

Been there, done more than you can dream
If you could only see the riddles defining
me
One push from the white light
One more calculated mistake
Shameless, running out of beings to blame
My company changes weekly
Another whore offering me something warm
Another sliver of me sacrificed
Boredom spins a frayed yarn
Needle point is redundant to me
That you miss that shows you don't
understand
Wasted face in a wasteland
Blends in
Always whatever the situation calls for
Walk in, stroll out
Such a con
Share the wealth
To share a bed
There's no way to fuck it all away
I can't even remember the names
Maybe it's easier this way
Tired of being romantic
But I can't shake the hopeless part
Collecting pounds of flesh
Breathing in the decay
This is my life
Why the fuck do you pretend you want to
stay?

8-30-2001

Essay in Futility

Ended it.
Dreaming what it was like to hold you, feel
your warm touch
On my weathered skin
Love you in a moment.
Let's begin it.
Need life back, in the worst way. Lust is
trust.
Want life back in my arms in the worst way.
Peel back the selfishness and paint on the
make ups.
Emptiness is a crowded place to hang out
Mirror staring is a tired way to pass my
time
Reflections distorted by hatred
Take down my name and number, but just be
sure to leave a message
Because I don't go home
World seen through new found deceptions
Blend me in, weary off the splash she makes
It's beauty, creature of habit drink some
pleasure for the time being
Grind, grind, yeah, that's a fine way to
unwind
Peeping in my window, All a cagey
distraction
But that is the thing, animal attraction,
benign satisfaction
I distort emotion, I crowd evil into the
ether
And for tonight, you and I can sleep
entwined as one

And tomorrow we'll be done.
Somehow think my purity resides in sin,
humility drips arrogance
While blood keeps seeping out the faucet....

UNKNOWN DATE

High Coos a.k.a. See What I Did?

Pain wears beauty well
Still grasping for sanity
On slippery flesh

Needle jockey whips
Deliver the lie on time
Every today fades

She's a diamond soul
Extended credit waning
Her flesh the rapture

Exhumed

I gladly swallow the tapeworm I am fed
Not some get over on me thing
I allowed it inside
To waste my nourishment
Force fed some parasitic decay
My flesh my sustenance
Weakening
Deteriorating
Day by day
Wasting
Fatigue chokes Fear swarms
I allowed it inside
Offer my soul
For her
Fatten up
Because I would give her anything
And I already have
My head running on empty
My heart pumping shards of glass
Spirit ground down to dust
All of it hers
Throwing everything at the moon
Hoping a beam radiates the blackness
Illuminates the hole in my heart
So I know where to stitch it up
Spin my dreams
The teetering top
Weeble wobble reality
When all I want is to fall the fuck down
Gave you everything
Use me up for some twisted creation
Take comfort in this new found damnation

Moving Picture Shows

Boredom...
Like watching turtles on barbiturates fuck
in Antarctica
Sitting on a porch watching grandma knit
and battle senility

What comes out is 2 fingered glove for a
non-existent grandson
Life on a dime rarely turns into a dollar
When it does the memories seemed etched in
dust

And so it goes...
Back to the monotony
Where snails cross salt flats
And the birds eat the bees
Time for the dreams to roll up their sleeves
Put in a dishonest day's work
Petition for longer nights for some
increased debauchery
Anything to bust up existence's tedium

Excitement...
Searching for some
Indiana Jones type adventure
Zzzzzz...
Instead rolling boulders in my mind
Crush my will
So I conclude this...
Feeding some turtles Seconals & Ecstasy
And filling up the tub with a lot of ice
Setting up the camcorder for time lapse

This is going to be awesome...

9-12-2000

Intoxicated Ramblings aka Little Debbie

Hey there, yes you.
You look so fucking incredible.
What's your name?
Slips through me cause I'm so distracted,
Attracted to the flesh.
No purse, so where's the ID. ?
My plan is unraveling,
My mind is space traveling.
I'm more creative in your verbatim.
I think it was, "Fuck me from behind & I'm
yours."
And the pot of gold isn't at the end of the
rainbow,
It's in the slit, suck me in and drown me.
I let you get me high, needle to the vein
The juice is sweet, the nectar of the gods.
I eat you, I relish you, I fuck you.
The chairs are rearranged and so I fall
down.
I admit it, it was comically ugly.
Fucking you was pure lust and so right.
What's your name, I'm offended.
I know you are so sexy that I'm coming
already except I'm a million miles away
So I'll call you Janine, does that make it
better?

I knew we'd not be 1 tonight, so I'm
obliterated.
But I know you want me as you fuck him.
Feel it deep.
Fuck me hard.
I'm yours, as long as I'm inside you.
Conditional love rules this tainted world.
So I just live for now, for your flesh's
burn..
Perfect sin.
I'm in.

I Forgot the Cheez Whiz aka Words Don't Do Her Justice

A dream
Realized
Sculpted splendor
Fortunate to share her light
An ocean sunrise
Pales next to her beauty
Everything just right
Forgotten souls
Remember each other
Now and forever
Feeling life
Catch for the first time
Life in focus
With her next to me
Cumbersome existence
Transformed into celestial purpose

With just one kiss of those lips
Eyes transfixed
A moment of pleasure
Loops
Into eternal reality
Look at heaven
And wonder how
I got so lucky
To hold this loveliness
Close to me
This angel that sees
Beauty through
The ugliness that was me
Carries me higher
Than substance ever took me
A pause-
Time to reflect
On this perfection
Whom I am giving my everything
Her heart is where I belong
Her love completes
The journey
She is the only place
I want to be...

8/20/2007

Posthumous Autobiography

He's back on the pixie dust
Watch out
Heed the warning
His head is all out of whack
He's talking grandiose
He's walking on water on his hands
Taking out your insecurities
Repo'ed all your dreams
He's becoming a revolution
An existential carousel
With bad intentions
Taking numbers without names
Breaking spines and clipping souls
He's speaking in tongues
Pushing fate into your path
Unlawful breeding
No license required for this skill
Pull a cause out of the closet
Find something worth dying for
Before it's too late
Because I know him
I made the mistake of waking him up
Now he is me

The
Hidden
Hairy
Austrian

Found Einstein
Hiding in the cabinet
Under my sink
With the bleach & toilet paper
Pulled him out of my mind
Shoved him into reality
Together we played with time
Hatched relativity
He wanted all the credit
And got the fanfare
He deserved neither
And got just that
Once I discovered his secret place
Armed with cosmic cutlery
I embarked on my journey
To swing the blade
Send ripples through time
Pulling the future back
Pushing the past forward
Where it won't much matter
I had to create this masterpiece
Cut and splice memories
To give me a future
Secure it forever
Chose my subject
The moment when passion sparked
Mix it up
Into my arms she falls
Perfect in every way

See a bit of danger in what comes next
The moment when I freeze the feeling
Dub it & put it on an eternal loop
Love unchanged in a world out of control
We are the only constant
For now
I might just get this right
All because one night I had the vision
Of Einstein and time
Trapped under my sink

7-19-2001

Dips

There's something special about her
guacamole, maybe it's the avocadoes she
picks from her trees, the cilantro she snips
from the garden. I admire her attention to
detail, down to her passion for composting
all her scraps because to me it's special
decay produces growth.

We take her guac everywhere, tonight
smuggled into the opera, Wagner demands it,
and it takes some real talent given her
tight red evening gown and tiny clutch.
She's graceful in her deceit, while I try not
to break the chips under my suit jacket.
Brings back those glory days of drug
running, bolos made me as notorious as

Biggie. Grandiosity suits me, like medieval armor, so let me run with half-truths which honestly are lies, but I like to twist words figuratively, digression...sorry. Why were the police on the lookout for me? Seems I pull the feathers from peacocks and leave them without any way to attract a mate or ward off predators with plumage- maybe that's a poor analogy since I have no frame of practical reference when it comes to vibrant plumes of that particular fowl.

This is what happens when you bake cookies in the furnace and heat the house with the oven- things just don't turn out write, intentional, right? I get I pursue folly religiously, which is kind of funny in its own form of validity, no one expects the Spanish Inquisition after all, but getting back to the crux, it's hard to time tortilla crunches with crescendos while I question why I am huffing ether through a gasmask, all the while craving sleep and a damp towel to wipe off the stain from my faux tuxedo life.

Winter Coat

Razor blade traces my vein.
Blood masks the path.
Dizziness obscures my consciousness.
Disturbed art, beauty in my finality.
At least I think so.
Miss me?
Well, I miss you too.
Every lonely breath,
Every empty promise.
Is there pain in my violence?
Is there sadness in my self-inflicted
madness?
Cold comfort exhausts my gravest memories.
Each heartbeat spills more of my life.
More of my unwanted love.
Covered.

Words Jump

Brain Freeze.
Function Tease.
Release.
Peace.
Ebb.
Flow.
Rest.
Finish.
Hope. Ruins.
Digest. Regrets.
Upset the rest.
Tide. Low.
Tide. High.
Tide. Quit.
Something fights for nothing.
Happy to win that war.
Slows.
Run.
Walk.
Crawl.
No movement at all.
Defeat.
Perception.
Victorious.
Jealousy.
Smiles.

PART 2:
SWEAT

Poetry lies itself to truth.
-John Ciardi

Timed Detonation

Spent my night in a conscious dream
Peeling my skin off to come clean
Elaborate set up of incense and fire
Vain attempts to force my mind to tire
Did you want me to fall this far down?
Push me into your soul to watch me drown
Allowed you to feed off my spirit
Talking with death cause I don't fear it
Respond ASAP to my invitation
Fueling this fantasy is my salvation
Watching the ink dry
Eyes have nothing left to cry
Immaculate vision of profound disgrace
Seems my pride has been misplaced
Picking up pieces of my flesh
Still taste you so close to death
My feet aren't even touching the ground
Funny how my spine snaps without a sound
You are the ultimate breakdown in sanity
Always a sucker for flesh with such vanity
Sad attempt at excising the demon I've
become
Why do I think all this pain is tons of fun?
So comfortable trapped in this despair
Always known I am too fucked up for repair
So just sweep the pieces of me off your mind
Just know I will love you for all of time

Hairline Fractures

Damage hits the 5th degree with the words
that roll from her tongue
Seemingly effortless, yet well thought out
Wonder if she rehearsed her lines...
Did she have a writer and dialog coach
Or do I just inspire hatred
Maybe I am like milk...passed my expiration
date
"We have to break up so I don't cheat on
you."
Excuse me?
Nonchalant, gutting me with a rusted steak
knife would feel better
Just like that she's gone
Just like that I am unsteady
Teetering on the brink
Seems my sanity sprung a leak
No little Dutch folk to put in finger in
the dam
Or is it dyke?
What's the difference
These people crashed their economy over
tulip bulbs
Whereas I collapse over some love
Science calls it a bump up in serotonin and
dopamine
Dope in me
Dope is me
No matter because my emotions have been
sucked out
She is my black hole, my succubus and I got
to say-

I want her back
Not to reconcile, but so she can rubberneck,
gaze at my wreckage
Slip in the blood to see me face to face
She built me up and now I need to tear her
down
Force feed understanding
Choke on the grief, take my hand
I want you to suffer, inject some infection
straight to the vein
A perfectly created bug, takes her down
slowly
Feel the demise, cell by cell, decay
uninterrupted
No prayers or pleas will stop it, sleep a
long forgotten luxury
The pain never fades, constant high tides,
wave after wave breaks
Beg me to end it, and I tell her something,
just unrehearsed,
A bit unpolished-
"I can't shatter anymore of you, because I
used up all of you. But here's a gun if you
want to end it though. I am not a complete
ass hole, not leaving you completely high
and dry."
Give her an exit but only when she is too
weak to stand
Unless of course she wants me back
And then I mean absolutely none of this

Prison Blues With a Bit of a Kick

Lights out, already time is a ghost.
Life suddenly a bit too utilitarian
Concrete blocks and a whole lot of steal,
some metal too.
Just don't tell me I can't spell, grew up in
Pittsburgh for Gods' sake!
Now that all that is cleared up, something
is creeping up

29 going on 103, stainless, *sans* seat toilet,
they have to be kidding.
Ponder what is going to hit me first, when
my stomach twists
Bologna and cheese is just as bad coming up,
take my word for it
All of this
It just is not worth it, euphoric I am not
The past 2 weeks of 'nourishment' have
decided they are tired of the view
This is not real, I am not in jail, not dope
sick, caged
With the temperature at 60, gives new
meaning to cold turkey
My mind is everywhere, did I talk to my
parents on my birthday?
Should I make that phone call, can I
deliver a new level of disappointment
Rock bottom...well Sherlock, there's this
shit called dynamite.
Compressed air and jack hammers
All that is going on inside my brain
anyway,

The shakes, the sweats, muscles cramp
Fear rapes the last shred of dignity,
Trapped
Criminal
Sick
Body aches, and then it really digs in.
No sleep as I toss and turn, agony forcing
me to scream "Fuck"
Someone is going to stab me
No way everyone is not hearing me cry out
The electric eel doubling as my spine
Can't...
Lie...
Still.
Kind of ironic...
Master manipulator, skillful deceiver
The compliments thrown out on my way to the
airport
Left everything behind me
Except my toughest enemy
The one finding these words
The thing that is craving more
"We can always dig the (w)hole deeper."

10/10/10 Poem
Aka Transcendental Communion

Exponential beauty
A futile explanation
Words don't exist
Every feeling building
Most complete union
Mind, body and spirit
6 entities fuse into one
One perfect expression
Of the ultimate love

Intelligent grace
Gorgeous kindness
Celestial wisdom

Every cell ignites
At the slightest touch
Feel her skin from miles away
The warmth inside her
Deep penetrating
Stares
Minds twist
As our bodies slip
Into one another
Intimate expressions
Slow and hard pressed
Wet and tight
Souls follow our
Flesh's puzzle piece fit
Sweat drips
Tongues dance
The world shakes

And only she exists
Just her and I
Purest connection
Every plane visited
Cherished sensation
Tattooed on my brain

These words fail
Can't convey heaven
Limited vocabulary
When it comes to this
Love
Craving, longing
For just another minute
Of her company
To hear her voice
To feel her breath
To touch her skin
Listen to her mind
Tomorrow can never
Get here quick enough
When we will be together
Back at the beginning again

PRETTY PAIN PENSIONERS

Tried to walk towards the light,
The shadows the past casts drown my sight
Every fighter loses the will to press
further
I'd reach my hand out if someone were there
A little too tainted to touch
The big nothing on the scale of something's
Remembering those promises she swore were
etched in cement
Watching the waves roll on shore
Love just that easy to erase
Run, far and fast, don't want my
imperfections weighing on any consciences
Let me protect everyone's innocence since I
lack my own
Wish I could say I was everyone's favorite
fading fleck
That face in the photo, behind humanity's
cheese forced smiles
Admission that I was someone
Someone still right here
The mix of scars, scabs, blood and infection
She keeps me secret, my existence her dirty
surreptitious enigma
I deliver the goods, pack the heat and
amaze
Just to heighten the level of
disappointments that come along with the
package
Sleights of tongue and twists of faith
Where is everyone
All of that forever, eternal love

Seems to expire after opening
This is me- the best guy you wish you never knew

Something different:

I preface all this by saying: she's my temptation, she holds judgment while my sins await adjudication. I'm wrapped up in the elusive dream, her flesh fantasy in reality has my morality bending. Those eyes, oceans in which I'm comfortably drowning.

I met her one night at the beach, two strangers wishing on dying stars, asked her with point blank corniness,
"Are you my wish answered?"
"I was going to ask you the same thing, but it was too hokey, at least we agree on something already."
That's how it began, so entranced by fate, I was willing to ride our spiral down to the day in death we would forcibly part. My soul endured lacerations at her hands, it just didn't matter to me. I'd kiss her feet, and I get you don't understand.

You can't slice a potato with a tomahawk, will never be thin enough to see through or deep fry crisp.

My sunsets some consider tainted purple, all alone in the vacuum of her absent beauty. Staring at the night sky is different now, every dying star isn't so much shooting as fading. It makes me remember though, I've come so far, seeing ugly can birth exquisite and pain certainly delivers pleasure.

Random Fragment of My Imagination

Still see you walk out the door
Nothing really changes
No glance back over the shoulder
Maybe because we feel we'll meet again
Some distant day
A distraction forcing reminiscence
My skin feels your touch and goose bumps leap

But that isn't how it is, is it?
We're gone, and I move on
Unwillingly, allowing the waves of fate to take me out
Far away, until we're specks on the fading horizon
I need this, so many outsiders praising me
Yet, I'd love to hear from you
My mind wrapped around my finger

PART 3:
Tears in Sanity

The novel is born of disillusionment; the poem, of despair.

-Jose Bergamin

Who Forgot the Fucking Piñata?

Heckle the night
Snowed in hope
Crippled chances
With no place to park
Stare away
Into closed space
Flashbulb memory
Burned fuzzy
Blinded sunspot
Entity
Bleeds pain
Right past
The will to fight
Forgot your name
But not the cause
Unreachable
Caffeine blend
Skittish much
Survive on instinct
Slowed breaths
Make you pay
For all that selfishness
A star's light
Struggles its way
Into sight
Physics tells you
I am already dead
When the shine
Hits
In your mind's twilight
Cave in
Inevitable hollow

Hairline fractures
Spider web splits
Now the heart is shattered
Fragmented fires
And no marshmallows
To roast
I am not laughing
At this misfortune
Or the fact
You proved me right
Used to the abandonment
Issue
Pick a scar
To scab
Not curious where
Life left its keys
Selling self-worth
With a kiss
And a kick
Sucker punch
And time comes
Undone

8/7/2007

Drive-thru Sinners

You spin fate on your finger
Love sick from a dash of poison
Waiting for the aftershocks to cease
But the tremors keep coming
Promise me your world
Deliver me a cold pizza
Silence splits me in asymmetrical two
And the bigger me feeds
A hurt reactionary
Soothe an ego with flesh
Calloused pride leaves bodies piled
My heart closed for business
Suicidal emotions
Love hanging from the rack
Where torture felt right
Plead for peace
Or settle for insanity
Either one get me off
I'm not mad at you
Just want to make you feel
Something
For me
And hatred seems alright
With her next to me
10-22-2013

Faith

Gun shy love
Speak a volume
Take an hour
Out of today
Steal a heart
Crush a soul
Maintain your innocence
Watch the reaction
The sick fall
Fucks never random
Poison pure emotion
Weakened boy crawls
Over and over
Broken glass lust
False accusations sting
Freshly torn flesh
Never will mend
He goes back
Inside wicked warmth
Spread legged sanity
Wears patience thin
Damaged goods returned
Lead painted sins
Thanks for playing
Worshipping my routine
Burning personal hell
Offer dawn solutions
For dusk conditions

We both lose
Until we come
Back round again

12-12-12

Space Filler

Last minute ramblings, the sun sets on
another day I spend far away from truth.
Maybe it's easier to live like this, from a
distance even lies are fuzzy enough to be
mistakenly identified. Optical illusions
confound, my faith tired of coming unwound.

Sometimes letting the one you love is the
best thing. Time tells it's stories in
retrospect, because blow by blow doesn't
always have all the facts straight.

It doesn't mean I won't remember all the
great times, but it does signify I can't add
anything else to the story when you are
busy writing your own endings.

Liberty City

Winter chill in the summer air
Treading down those numbered streets
Autopilot awareness seeing it all
Every step a fracture in my sanity

Self-imposed slavery
Some bullshit happiness
Keeps me in chains
Tightness loosening, train is coming

Broken down, weary, bleary
That corner market savior
False profit beauty
Another rape of consciousness

Brown-eyed smiles
Soulless imagination
Something better than…
This?

Nagging gnawing won't shut up
Something not allowing my today
To forget all the yesterdays
Skipping time so tomorrow is now

The same choke
Spit stones at me
Curse my touch
The leech sucks us dry

Sunken, shallow
Bended knee snapping

Lift a hand up
Or curl up and die?

Every push
Deepens the hole
Darkened dreams
Is this hello or goodbye?

5/31/2011

Jen's Poem

You are the first beam of light through the
blinds
The one that tears open the darkness
Its brilliance sparks my heart
The ray's warmth mimics a kiss from your
lips
A path to happiness illuminated in ocean
blue eyes

You are that first breath when I awake
The air clean, sustaining and pure
A hint of your perfume caught in that
moment
Close my eyes, see you right next to me
The taste of your skin is here

Even while you are not
A breeze slides across my skin
A beautiful reminder of your soft touch

You are my steps through the day
Sometimes as a memory to put shatter
personal doubt
Or to break through a visiting, suffocating
thought
I can trace the beauty of your face
Sculpt the gorgeous curves of your body
And paint today classic
I am truly in earth bound heaven, you right
next to me
We cheat gravity, we float hand in hand
The most magnificent ones
We disappear from the billions
Alone in perfection
Kissing, loving in the setting sun

You are the heavens
Each star a piece of our puzzle
A full moon guiding us into each other's
arms
You are bright, brilliant and radiant
My nightly prayer, my peace and love
You are an angel in a world of slaves
Unique on a planet of conformity

You are the grandest of dreams
An ember that lit the fire, scintillating

from afar
Pure dazzle in your presence
You are love - pure and passionate
An emotion indescribable
It's understanding, tender and unbreakable
Goes way beyond my wildest imagination
Shatters every past conception
It is my strength...it makes me want to see
tomorrow
To see that first ray of light

You are everything
You are my love, held fast and tight
A perfect balance of inner and outer
beauties
An unyielding kindness, that warms my soul
You feel like destiny when I hold you close
You are heaven when our bodies unite
You are once in a lifetime
And I treasure and cherish every second of
it
Because in you, all the pain dies.
 In you I am truly alive
4/15/12

STYLIZED STYPTIC PENCILS

PEDDLE ME...
NEWPORTS AND FORTIES
GRILLS AND RIMS
DRUGS AND SPORTS
RAP DREAMS AND IMPARTIAL GENOCIDE
BIGMAC EXPLOITATION NO ONE SEES
A LANGUAGE OF MY OWN
TO COMPLETE MY UNIQUENESS-
EQUALITY THROUGH DIVISION AND
SEPARATION

RAISE ME...
SINGLE PARENT DISASTER
WITH AN MTV FATHER
AND A PS3 EDUCATION
MYSPACE NIGHTS AND A BOX OF TWINKIES
LAZY LONELINESS DOMINATES
FEELING EMO
GRAB A TATTOO AND EYE SHADOW
HOT TOPIC CAREER GOALS
STAND APART - THE REBEL
DO EVERYTHING THE MEDIA TELLS ME-
BLENDING INTO THE DEFINED
MISUNDERSTOOD

BLIND ME...
WITH SEX AND CHILD LABOR
WIDER PROFITS FOR A NARROWER FEW
A CHEAP LAUNDRY BASKET
$10 DISHES AND $5 FLATWARE
WALMART OPPORTUNITIES SLICE
THE LOCAL BUSINESS TO THE BONE

STARBUCKS LATTES AND OUT OF VASELINE
AND MY PARTICIPATION
MEANS ITS COOL WITH ME

SAVE ME...
WITH YOUR RELIGIOUS RIGHTEOUSNESS
SUNDAY MORNING CHRISTIANS
MAKES 6-DAY SINNERS ALRIGHT
MIND CONTROL WHACK JOBS
WHILE THE CHURCH ANGELIC LEADERS
FALL INTO WHORES' ARMS
UNDER COVER OF NIGHT
"LOVE EVERYONE" – A GUY NAMED JESUS
(UNLESS THEY AREN'T A MEMBER) – NOT JESUS
"TREAT EVERYONE AS YOU WANT TREATED" –
AGAIN, THAT JESUS GUY
(UNLESS THEY ARE GETTING ABORTIONS) –
NOT JESUS
COMPLICATE THE SIMPLE
AFTER ALL, GOD IS GOOD BUSINESS

TYPECAST ME...
AMERICAN
HOUSE POOR, HUMMER DRIVING
PHARMACEUTICAL SOLUTION SEEKER
TV...TV...STATUS
SALINE IMPLANTATION
AND ALL IS FINE
UNTIL THE APR GOES UP 1%
AND MY CREDIT CARDS MAX
PAYCHECK TO PAYCHECK
DEFINES THIS GAME
WAITING ON A LAWSUIT TO COME MY WAY

FREE ME...
FROM THE HERD
FREE WILL, OPEN MINDS
SELF-TAUGHT, QUESTION EVERYTHING
ESPECIALLY THOSE RAISING ALL THE
QUESTIONS
DO RIGHT...ALL THE TIME
BUILD A FAMILY, DISSECT THE ROTTING
DREAM
DISMANTLE THE MACHINE
RAISE YOUR HEAD, SPEAK YOUR MIND
DO YOUR PART
EVERY DAY
AND AMERICA WILL BE WHAT IS WAS MEANT TO
BE

Sleepless Thoughts

Blue-lipped dreamer with the 10-ton Chest
Confess my sins for one more breath
Rubber Soul watching the truth bounce
4 day brown out for just one ounce
Broken screams fall short
drifting away from port

Suicidal bliss mixed in her kiss
Uneasy at simply being
Pushing vacancies out of my mind
Been chewing my gristle for some time

Into the great white lie
My feet have left the ground

Penniless vagabond
Lifting veils off the sun
Watch the beams penetrate the haze
Thick around my mind
Sludge puddles evaporate
Hoping to find a bit of life in the dirt
Or at least a clue
To answer the only question
That will ever matter
Love and I
Was it lost, can it be found?
Questions have answers
No wonder I hate riddles
Even though I like to say conundrum
And Walla Walla...Pismo Beach
Clues...
Seriously weird how that my subconscious
Drives my past inside my present
Maybe it's better to be all alone
Just sucks to have no home

6-21-12

Loss of Balance

Dig that stiletto lust into my flesh
Dormant doormat dreamer defines me
Call me clever, call me, again
Fade outs and fade ins
A moment of flesh penetrates
The surface tension
Exhaustive research on the matter
Of fact causes to these reactions
Fear fuck a fantasy
My eyes are the window to my soul
Deep browns just about black
Buy a ticket to the show
I entertain a select few
Retreat because I don't want pushed
Into the arms of the next in line
Maybe know a thing about needles in the
hay
Light the bale on fire
Look at the remains
Sterilized and tempered
I close my eyes
Pray for a dream
Endure the nightmare
Watch dawn spread over another day
Allow gravity to exert force
As I fall away

2/1/15

I Am

I am at your disposal.
I'm whatever you need me to be.
I'm your lover, I'm your abuser.
I'm your affair, I'm your despair.
I'm a fucker, I'm a connection.
I'll get you high, I'll drive you low.
I've existed for everyone else's desires.
I'm a fucking chameleon.
You don't see me for what I really am.
You can't because I don't have a fucking
clue.
I flatter, I fuck, I hurt, I erase.
I calm I listen, I scream, I use.
I'll help you over him.
I'll let you get over on me.

I'll make your pain dissipate.
n me, it evaporates.
I'm the tourniquet on your soul.
I'm the man your parents forbid you to see.
I'm an addict, I'm your slave.
Use me, abuse me, take whatever you need.
I'll be o.k., honest. You needn't worry about
me!

Chorus:
I am your scabs
Your itch
Your pick

The infection breeds
Fulfill all your needs

7-21-12

Random Prose
Creation wasn't a big bang, just God
exhaling some wad of celestial phlegm,
infinite and somehow still beautiful. While
my nighttime medicated lungs, ok, 24-hour a
day suppressed lungs, strain to cough up
blood streaked snot, his was a rainbow, with
the sun our pot of gold, and everything else
in between his lips and the spit trail of
that logy proved perfection.

So I have to wonder, how do I fit into the
mix? I feel ancient, far removed from this
Wi-Fi enamored society, focused on
liquefied dinosaur decay, the black gold,
Jed move away from here, lie. That icecap
melting endgame folly of mankind. I'm too
astute for my own good, so I swallow more
lithium to even out my sanity, my wick's
burned each end but the slow burns
eventually collide. Maybe the pool of semi-
solid wax can fill in the void buried deep,
where rigs drill, and disappointment
breeds.

Once again, my bullshit astounds even me.

Cryogenic Perspectives

Clear sky dreamer
Faithful through the rolling grays
A littered past
Stabbing debris
Filing it away
My trash is only my treasure
Don't need to see past me
Because I'm looking you in the eyes
The always were's are never mores
Something to be said for dropping
victimology
Enough written about others
Filling in the blanks of self
Never was about heroin(e)
My own hero
The gifts too numerous
Peace is my happiness

11/26/2014

ABOUT THE AUTHOR

Michael Janflone was born south of Pittsburgh, in Washington, PA. He calls Delray Beach, FL home now, especially Off the Ave, the local Steelers bar during football season. He hates writing these, which if you read the back cover, you already know, so he must not be afraid of being redundant.

Shoestring Theories will be released very soon. All future and current as well as the past I guess, happenings can be followed via: http://flone73.wordpress.com

www.ingramcontent.com/pod-product-compliance
Lightning Source LLC
Chambersburg PA
CBHW071104040426
42443CB00013B/3395

9 780692 202326